HORRIBLE HISTORIES

DUBLIN

TERRY DEARY

Illustrated by Mike Phillips

■SCHOLASTIC

Scholastic Children's Books
Euston House, 24 Eversholt Street,
London, NW1 1DB, UK

A division of Scholastic Ltd
London ~ New York ~ Toronto ~ Sydney ~ Auckland
Mexico City ~ New Delhi ~ Hong Kong

Published in the UK by Scholastic Ltd, 2006

Text copyright © Terry Deary 2006
Illustrations copyright © Mike Phillips 2006
Cover illustration © Martin Brown 2006

10 digit ISBN: 0 439 95468 1
13 digit ISBN: 978 0439 95468 6

Printed by Nørhaven Paperback A/S, Denmark

4 6 8 10 9 7 5 3

The right of Terry Deary and Mike Phillips to be identified as
the author and illustrator of this work respectively has been asserted by
them in accordance with the Copyright, Designs and Patents Act, 1988.

Papers used by Scholastic Children's Books are made from wood grown in sustainable forests.

CONTENTS

Introduction

Lots of large towns and cities have their own songs.

Dublin even has a statue of the woman in its song, Molly Malone.

She was supposed to be the daughter of a fish-seller and took her shellfish through the Dublin streets to sell.

The song goes…

IN DUBLIN'S FAIR CITY
WHERE THE GIRLS ARE SO PRETTY
I FIRST SET MY EYES ON
SWEET MOLLY MALONE

AS SHE WHEELED HER WHEELBARROW
THROUGH STREETS BROAD AND NARROW
CRYING COCKLES AND MUSSELS
ALIVE, ALIVE OH!

Molly was also famous for being a bit of a flirt. But Molly, they say, died in 1699 of typhoid from drinking the filthy Dublin water (not from eating a rotten cockle). She was just 36 years old.

Mouldy Molly was buried in St John's Graveyard near Fishamble Street where she lived. The song ends…

> SHE DIED OF A FEVER AND NO ONE COULD SAVE HER AND THAT WAS THE END OF SWEET MOLLY MALONE. BUT HER GHOST WHEELS HER BARROW THROUGH STREETS BROAD AND NARROW CRYING COCKLES AND MUSSELS ALIVE, ALIVE OH!

But is Molly's story TRUE?

What you need is a horrible historian to tell you a few foul facts about the legend of Molly…

> MOLLY MALONE PROBABLY NEVER EXISTED

> BUT HER DEATH'S WRITTEN DOWN IN ST JOHN'S CHURCH RECORDS!

Lots of Mary Malones[1] were born and died in Dublin. No one can prove the fat fish-seller was one of them. If she was buried in St John's church we'll never know now – Dublin council dug up the graveyard to build some new council offices. The bones were scattered all over St John's Lane!

1 The nickname for Mary is 'Molly' – so some Mary Malones are called Molly Malone … and a lot are called Mary Malone. If you are called Ann Smith then you are not called either.

You see you can't believe all the stories they tell about Dublin. What you need is a book that will tell you the terrible truth, not the tittle-tattle and tales.

I'm glad you asked. Read on…

Early Dublin Timeline

300 BC The Cut-throat Celts arrive in Ireland and the different tribes share it out ... or fight it out.

AD 150 Irish leader 'Conn of the Hundred Battles' agrees to share Ireland with his old rival Mogh of Munster. The dividing line between their two shares starts in Galway and ends up at Dublin High Street. Crafty Conn gets handy Dublin harbour.

AD 432 St Patrick arrives in Ireland to preach Christianity. He passes through Dublin and the people there moan about the black water. St Pat makes a spring of fresh water spout out of the ground. Much later, St Patrick's Cathedral (in Patrick Street) was built on the spot.

AD 795 The first Viking invaders arrive in Ireland. The monks learn how to build high, round towers as look-out posts and for shelter. The Vikings rob then go home.

AD 831 The Vikings are back and this time they plan to stay. King Thorgest and his men settle down in County Louth and build the first city of Dublin. The Irish kings are too busy fighting each other to stop him.

The Vikings build a fortress in 840 (probably where the Castle is now). AD **944** Olaf 'Cuaran' becomes King of Dublin State. A new wave of Viking invaders begin to marry the Irish girls.

AD **980** King Olaf is attacked by Malachy from the north and runs off home. Brian Boru rules in the south while the Vikings hang on in Wexford, Waterford and Dublin.

1014 Brian Boru defeats the Vikings at the battle of Clontarf – then gets himself murdered. Malachy becomes the new Great King of Ireland but can't stop all the squabbles.

I'VE A LIKING FOR A VIKING!

I LIKE STRIKING A VIKING WHY KING?

Malachy ROOLS

VIKING DUBLIN

Around AD 500 most of Europe was in the 'Dark Ages' so called because we're 'in the dark' about what went on. Not many people were writing history. But Ireland was in a Golden Age. The monks were building wonderful monasteries and sending people out to preach to the rest of the world.

The horrible trouble is there is always someone that wants to spoil the party. They see a rich church and they don't say…

They say:

In AD 787 the Vikings began attacking monasteries in England. When there was nothing left to pinch they sailed round to Ireland and started mugging monks over there.

They found the town of Dublin was a great place to settle because it had a deep harbour.

Dublin takes its name from two Irish words, *dubh* and *linn*, which mean 'the black pool'. So Dublin is Ireland's answer to Blackpool – without the Blackpool Tower[2].

The river Liffey runs through Dublin and it is turned black by the marshes (peat bogs) it runs through. Still, this deep pool made a great harbour for Viking ships and Dublin was born.

Thorgest thumped

The Vikings were supposed to be sneaky and use tricks like ambushes against their enemies. The Irish were supposed to be good sports who liked to fight fairly. But they didn't fight very fair when it came to getting rid of the first Viking chief, Thorgest.

Here's what happened…

Once upon a time there was a lovely Irish girl whose name we don't know. So we won't tell you what it is. Anyway, the Viking warrior Thorgest fell madly in love with the girl and he probably knew her name! 'Let's have a party in my castle tonight, lovely Irish girl. I'll bring a few of my warriors and you bring some of your lovely girl friends to keep them company,' Thorgest said.

2 If you want to see the river's old black pool then it's now under Capel Street Bridge. Just don't look for Blackpool beach or jump in for a swim.

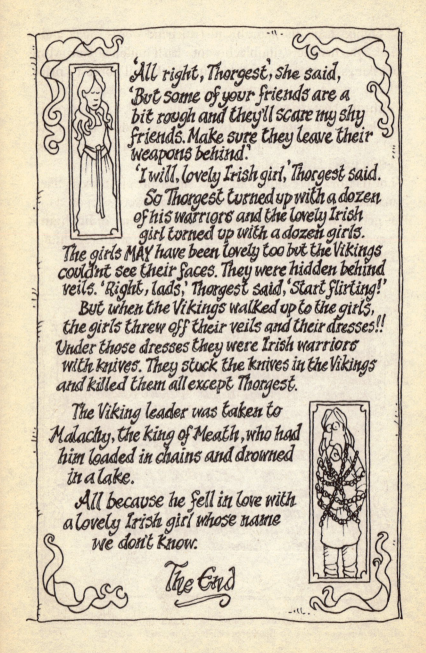

'All right, Thorgest', she said, 'But some of your friends are a bit rough and they'll scare my shy friends. Make sure they leave their weapons behind'.

'I will, lovely Irish girl', Thorgest said.

So Thorgest turned up with a dozen of his warriors and the lovely Irish girl turned up with a dozen girls. The girls MAY have been lovely too but the Vikings couldn't see their faces. They were hidden behind veils. 'Right, lads,' Thorgest said, 'Start flirting!'

But when the Vikings walked up to the girls, the girls threw off their veils and their dresses!! Under those dresses they were Irish warriors with knives. They stuck the knives in the Vikings and killed them all except Thorgest.

The Viking leader was taken to Malachy, the king of Meath, who had him loaded in chains and drowned in a lake.

All because he fell in love with a lovely Irish girl whose name we don't know.

The End

Nice story, but probably just a legend.

The massacre didn't do the Irish much good. More Vikings swarmed into Dublin to take thick Thorgest's place.

Dark Age daftness

The main Viking city in Ireland in the 800s and 900s was Dublin. Outside Dublin there were over a hundred Irish tribes and Viking villages.

In time the Vikings and the Irish people mixed. They squabbled, they married and made friends.

The Irish warriors learned a lot from their Viking neighbours. They learned to be killers and were called 'Sons of Death'.

Here are a few things you may NOT like to try if you go to Dublin today … because you'll be arrested.

13

Killing in Connaught became a sort of habit ... like going to Blackpool in summer if you want a holiday.

the Blood-dripping battle of clontarf

Of all the battles fought around Dublin the Battle of Clontarf in 1014 was the most important.

Before the battle the Vikings ruled, but the Irish grew strong enough to fight back. Dublin was the battleground. The Vikings weren't exactly driven out of Dublin and Ireland after the battle, but they were never as strong again. The Irish, led by Brian Boru, won – but it cost a lot of blood and a lot of lives.

Cruel Clontarf horrible fact file

1 One of the Viking leaders was Brodir. The Irish said he was a Christian 'magician'. His hair was so long he had to tuck it in his belt. He wore magical armour that no weapon could get through.
2 When Brian Boru arrived at Clontarf the night before the battle, Brodir sailed off into the Irish sea. 'He's too scared to fight us!' Brian's men cheered. But it was a trick. As soon as it grew dark Brodir sailed back to Clontarf and landed.

3 Brodir chose to fight on 23 April 1014 because it was Good Friday. He knew that Christian King Brian wouldn't want to fight on such a holy day.

4 Brian himself didn't fight but he carried a cross in one hand and a sword in the other. (He was getting a bit old to fight, mind you.)

HOW AM I SUPPOSED TO HOLD MY BLOOMIN' WALKING STICK?

5 The battle was a little odd at first. The two sides didn't just charge and chop. They began by having single combat fights. One Viking leader fought one Irish leader as their men cheered – like a boxing match. Each man fell with his enemy's sword in his body and his enemy's hair clutched in his hands.

WISH THEY'D INVENT WIG GLUE

6 Viking leader Brodir was beaten and ran into the woods to hide. The Dublin Vikings ran for the safety of the town. Their friends who had arrived from the sea ran back to their ships. But the tide had come in and they were too tired to swim. Brian Boru's 15-year-old grandson Tordhelbach chased two Vikings into the ocean and dragged them under. He also managed to drown himself, which is a bit of a stupid thing to do.

7 Brian Boru's Irish army had beaten the Vikings but it wasn't over yet. Brodir had been hiding in the woods. He saw Brian Boru just outside the woods. Many of Brian's guards were chasing the last Vikings. Brian was on his knees, praying. At first Brodir didn't recognize his enemy and said, 'Priest, priest!' and walked away. But his friend, who had recognized Brian, shouted, 'King! King!'[3] and they turned back.

Brodir rushed at Brian and lopped off his head with one blow of his axe. He cried...

Now let man tell man that Brodir killed Brian.

Brodir was soon captured. Brian's brother gave orders for Brodir to die a s-l-o-w and painful death.

8 Not only did 6,000 men die, but most of their leaders died too. Clontarf was one of the bloodiest battles in Irish history. The monks who told the story said...

Blood dripped from the trees!

Oak soaked.

3 No, I have no idea why they said the words twice. Maybe the noise of the battle was so loud they didn't hear each other the first time. Or maybe they were such vile Vikings their ears were plugged with wax. Or make up some answer for yourself.

9 Viking Sygtrygg was safe inside his fortress in Dublin. He watched the battle with his mum beside him. He didn't go out to fight and wouldn't come out to fight the next day either. Can you blame him?

So the Irish army stripped the dead bodies of their weapons and left them for Sygtrygg's men to bury.

10 Brian Boru was dead, as was his grandson Tordhelbach and his son Murchad. Ireland was without a king. The Irish chiefs would spend years and lots of blood fighting each other. In time the Vikings married the Irish and became part of the Irish people. They're still there today – but they won't be waving axes and magic banners so it may be hard to spot them.

Did you know…?
If you want to see the place where Brian Boru got the chop then it is said to be in Mountjoy Square. His tent was there, they say. Don't worry, they've mopped up the blood.

Rotten raven banner

Another Viking leader, Sigurd, showed the Vikings a banner with a raven on it. It had been woven by his mother and it carried a curse. He explained…

But Sigurd kept quiet about the rest of the curse…

An Irish warrior killed the man carrying the banner so another Viking picked it up. He was killed too. Sigurd ordered one of his captains to pick it up, but another, the Viking Asmund the White, told the captain, 'You'll be killed if you do!' and the captain refused.

Finally Sigurd picked it up because if the banner was captured the battle was lost. He knew the risk. He tried to hide it under his cloak where the Irish couldn't see it.

Sigurd was killed with a spear.

Nice try, Sigurd.

But have you noticed the odd bit about the curse? The 'Follow the banner and win' curse didn't work – but the 'Hold the banner and die' curse DID!

Bloody Bram

Eight hundred and thirty three years after the blood-dripping battle at Clontarf a baby was born in the village where the battle had taken place.

The baby grew up to be the writer Bram Stoker.

Bram who? The man who wrote the blood-dripping book *Dracula*. Was there a link?

Dire Dubliners

If you could travel back in time there would be dire Dubliners to avoid. Find details of the 'Dublin people you wouldn't want to meet' (probably) throughout this book.

Here's the first one…

Dire Dubliners 1:
Brian Boru (940–1014)

Facts you need to know

• Brian ruled most of Ireland from 1002. He didn't just rule because he was a great warrior – he ruled by using some clever ideas and by making friends.

• Sygtrygg Silkbeard was leader of the Dublin Vikings and Brian Boru made friends with him by marrying Sygtrygg's mum, Gormlaith – he threw her in jail as soon as Sygtrygg started making trouble.

Facts you don't want to know

Brian used Viking warriors to fight for him. They raided Britain and robbed the west coast. Brian told the Irish…

I WANT YOU TO WELCOME THIS VIKING INTO YOUR HOME AS A GUEST. FEED HIM AND LOOK AFTER HIM AS IF HE WAS AN IRISH WARRIOR

ARE IRISH WARRIORS THAT SMELLY?

But in 1013 Brian had become powerful enough to attack the Dublin Vikings. He told his Irish people…

NOW I WANT YOU TO MURDER YOUR GUEST IN HIS SLEEP. AS SOON AS YOU HAVE DONE IT LIGHT A TORCH AND SHOW IT OUTSIDE YOUR HOUSE

RIGHT'O!

ZZZZZZZ

That night thousands of torches burned outside Irish homes.

Gory Gormlaith

If Brian could be a cruel avenger then one of his wives, Gormlaith, was worse.

Gormlaith was Trouble. Two kings had divorced her so Brian was the third to dump her. She was upset. And when Gormlaith was upset she only thought about one thing … revenge.

She sent out a message to Brian's Viking enemies…

WANTED

VIKING WARRIOR WITH GUTS

JOB:
KILL BRIAN BORU

REWARD:
The Viking who kills Boru will be
rewarded by being made

HIGH KING OF IRELAND

YES! YOU COULD HAVE A THRONE OF YOUR OWN!
Just kill the old man and win the prize of a
lifetime. It's an offer you can't refuse!!

Apply: To High Queen Gormlaith

Come on lads, what are you waiting for?

Please note: If you are not able to read
this poster then get a monk to read
it to you!

Would YOU have applied? No Viking did so you'd have probably got the job!

Horrible Histories odd fact: Everyone agrees Brian was killed at the Battle of Clontarf, near Dublin, while he was praying in his tent. The killer Brodir was captured, tortured and killed.

BUT ... another story says the Viking Brodir came into Brian's tent. King Brian Boru jumped to his feet and grabbed his sword.

With one stroke the King chopped through both the legs of the Viking. At the same moment the battle-axe of Brodir fell on the King's head. Each had killed the other.

This is VERY unlikely, of course. Getting the sword sweep and the head chop at the same time is probably impossible.

Horrible Histories warning: Do NOT try this at home to see if it can be done! Go to school and get a couple of history teachers to try it.

Middle Ages Dublin

The Vicious Vikings settled down around the 1100s. That's the good news. The bad news was that their cousins, the stormin' Normans, started the raiding and rampaging. It was only a matter of time before they brought their nasty Norman ways to Ireland and Dublin…

1170 The Normans are coming. They arrive at County Wexford, led by the Earl of Pembroke – his nickname is 'Strongbow'. They'll be off to Dublin soon. In 1171 they are being attacked by Viking King Hasculf's forces. By 1172 the Pope has said the Normans in England can rule Ireland[4]. The cheek of it!

1185 Prince John arrives from England. He upsets the Irish chieftains so much (find out how on page 62) they rebel and he has to build Dublin Castle to save his skin.

1308 Dublin gets a fresh water supply when the stream called the Dodder is piped across the fields and allowed to run down the main street! You can put a pipe into your house from the flowing gutter – but the pipe must be no wider than a goose feather.

1315 There's a Bruce on the loose but he's not a goose! Edward Bruce of Scotland invades and brings terror

---

4 Well, he was Pope Adrian IV and he was an Englishman. What do you expect?

to Ireland. But the people of Dublin keep him out so he has to go home.

1349 The plague arrives – the dreaded Black Death…

1366 The Statutes of Kilkenny are laws that say the Normans and the Irish must not trade with each other or marry each other. (Not even the women of Dublin City where the girls are so pretty.) Marry a Dublin girl and you are executed! (The law doesn't work.)

1385 Dublin Bridge has fallen down. The people have to cross the Liffey in boats.

1409 Dublin harbour is plagued by pirates. One gang captures a bishop but the loyal people chase the pirates down the river and get the bish back.

1467 The Earl of Desmond, the Irish governor, rebels and is found guilty of treason. King Edward IV is so upset he sends the Earl of Worcester to Dublin to stick Desmond's head on a spike at Dublin Castle. (Don't worry, it didn't hurt because it had been chopped off the day before.) He also had Desmond's infant sons killed – nasty[5].

5 Desmond was buried in Christ Church, Dublin. In 1570 the statue of Strongbow was kicked out to make way for a statue of dead Des. People look at the statue and say, 'Ooooh! That's the famous Strongbow who founded Christ Church. Fancy that!' But it's not. Poor old headless Des even has his headless name forgotten now. Make sure you say, 'Hello, Des!' if you go and see him. He'll like that.

Weird wedding custom

In the Middle Ages (around 1200 to 1500) there were only about 10,000 people in Dublin. You could walk from the city wall on one side to the city wall on the other in about nine minutes. And the city walls were so important they became part of Dublin weddings.

What did the bride and groom have to do after their wedding?

a) Give the wall a piece of wedding cake – it would go stale and hard after a few days and make the wall stronger.

b) Throw the bride's mother off the wall, into the Liffey as a sacrifice to keep the wall gods happy.

c) Kiss the wall for luck.

Answer: c) The mayor of Dublin would go to every wedding. After the church service he would lead the married couple to the city wall and there they would kiss it.

26

Naughty night girls

In Dublin in the Middle Ages the priests and the councillors were worried about women wandering around in the dark and chatting up the poor helpless men.

There were no street lights and the women could be luring the men into a trap where a big bad boyfriend could rob their victim.

In the dark there was one good way to attract the men – that was to call out. (I don't know what a wicked woman would call out to attract men … probably something like, 'Hello, handsome! Buy me a pint and I'll give you a cuddle!')

Anyway, the Dublin council passed a curious law to stop this hanky-panky…

They said that any woman found crying out after dark (without a good reason) would have all her clothes taken away from her on the spot!

Dire Dubliners 2: Dermot MacMurrough (1110–1171)

Facts you need to know

• Dermot, Irish King of Leinster, spent most of his life fighting against the Irish High King, Turlough O'Connor. In 1166 Dermot had to flee to England and was defeated again when he came back the next year.

• Dermot was REALLY upset with the people of Dublin because they had killed his father and buried him with a dead dog as an extra insult.

So in 1169 he invited an army led by Norman knights to help him. But Dermot's Dublin disaster turned out to be the biggest mistake in Irish history. Not only did the Normans help him capture Dublin in 1170 – they also helped themselves … to Irish land.

Facts you don't want to know

A lot of tales were told about Dermot's cruelty, but the stories were written by the Normans years after he was dead. They may not be true.

Still, this is a *Horrible Histories* book and you want to hear one or two, don't you?

When 16-year-old Dermot took the Leinster throne in 1126 there were 17 chieftains against him. He had some killed and the rest had their eyes put out.

Another horror story was that Dermot gathered a pile of enemy heads after a battle and spotted the head of a man he really hated. Dermot picked up the head. What did he do next?
a) spewed
b) chewed
c) glued

Answer: b) Dermot sank his teeth into the face and tore at it.

After Dermot's attack on Dublin, King Turlough took Dermot's son prisoner and in 1171 delivered him to Dermot in a sack.
Dead.

Dermot lost heart and died a few months later. But the Normans were there to stay. The bitter Irish have blamed Dermot ever since. They say Dermot did not die a natural death.

They say his flesh rotted off while he was still alive. When enough bits had dropped off he died.

Horrible Histories odd fact: Dermot spent years fighting the chieftain Tiernan O'Rourke. Finally, in 1152, he kidnapped Tiernan's wife … don't worry, she was really keen to run off with Dermot.

But what did Dermot pinch at the same time?

a) her bottom
b) her cattle
c) her furniture

Answer: b) and c) After a year he sent the wife back to Tiernan. Maybe he only loved her for her kitchen cabinet. Sad.

CRUEL CATHEDRALS

The cathedrals of Dublin are lovely to look at today. But some odd things have happened there in the past. Aren't you glad you weren't alive then? (Especially as you'd be dead now if you were alive then, so you wouldn't be able to read this book!)

St Patrick's Cathedral

Built on the place visited by St Patrick in AD 432 (see page 8), this cathedral is Dublin's oldest Christian site.

Most cathedrals have a 'crypt' under the floor – a large cellar, useful for storing old bodies. But not St Patrick's – if you tried to dig a cellar you'd be digging in water.

What is it about Dublin cathedrals? Christ Church was built on a bog and St Patrick's was built over a stream … the Poddle. This must have wrecked the summer holidays for Dublin kids:

THANKS PATRICK, NOW WE'LL NEVER PADDLE IN THE PUDDLES OF THE PODDLE AGAIN

BUT SEAMUS, WE NEVER PADDLED IN THE PODDLE PUDDLES AFTER YOU PIDDLED IN IT!

St Patrick's Cathedral came in very handy in 1316 when the Scots army of Edward Bruce invaded Ireland and marched on Dublin.

Did the people of Dublin rush to the abbey to pray?

No. They rushed to the abbey, ripped part of it down and used the stones to build a wall!

It was such a good wall the Scots gave up and attacked Limerick instead. Edward's army ran out of food and went home. He was killed in battle in 1318 and a quarter of his body was stuck on Dublin Castle on a pole.

Chance your arm

Not all fights in Dublin ended in death, of course.

In 1492 the Earl of Kildare and the Earl of Ormond had a big row in St Patrick's Cathedral. The cowardy-custard Earl of Ormond went off into a room called the Chapter House with his bodyguard and locked himself in.

The Earl of Kildare decided it was a bit of a daft argument and said...

The Earl of Ormond ignored this offer so the Earl of Kildare used a spear head to cut a square hole in the door. Then he took a great risk ... he stuck his arm through the door and said, 'Let's shake hands!'

That was chancing (or risking) his arm because the Earl of Ormond might well have chopped it off[7]. But the Earl of Ormond clasped the hand and shook it. He opened the door and the two men hugged one another.

If you go to St Patrick's Cathedral today you can see the very door with the hole cut out!

6 Yes, all right, he didn't exactly offer to 'kiss' the Earl of Ormond but you know what I mean.
7 No jokes about the Earl of Kildare being a pretty 'armless chap.

Dire Dubliners 3: Richard de Clare, Earl of Pembroke (known as 'Strongbow') d. 1176

Facts you need to know

Strongbow had lands in Wales but was happy to help Dermot MacMurrough to fight his enemies in Ireland. In 1169 Strongbow led an army into Ireland and fought for Dermot at Waterford. His reward was to get the hand of Dermot's daughter, Eva.

Facts you don't want to know

• As soon as Strongbow had won victory in Waterford he married Eva – probably in Waterford Cathedral.

But one report says they were married at the place where the city walls were broken. Their wedding took place in the middle of piles of bleeding corpses.

• Strongbow enjoyed being cruel. In May 1170 he attacked Waterford, and the Irish defenders rode out to attack his army. The Irish were beaten and 70 of their men captured. Strongbow could have held them prisoner or killed them quickly. He didn't.

First he took them to the cliff top and had their arms and legs broken. Then they were thrown into the sea.

It's hard to swim ashore when your arms and legs are broken.

• Strongbow was just as cruel to his own family, as this story shows…

Horrible Histories odd fact: In 1171 Strongbow was in Dublin, surrounded by a large Irish army who wanted to kill him. Strongbow took a force of just 600 knights and rode out to attack the Irish. Somehow they managed to scatter their Irish enemies. The Irish King wasn't there to lead his men.

Where was he? He was having a bath.

He had to make a run for it without his clothes.

Christ Church Cathedral

This cathedral was first built from wood by the Vikings, so of course it rotted. Strongbow the Norman came along and in 1172 started building a stone cathedral to take its place.

He died before it was finished and his insides were probably buried here.

But the nutty Normans had built that new stone cathedral on a bog. In 1562 it fell down and had to be rebuilt.

There is a tomb in the cathedral that is said to be an image of Strongbow. Beside it is half a statue of a young man. Some people believe this is the son that Strongbow sliced in two but *Horrible Histories* readers know better...

THIS IS STRONGBOW'S SON STANDING IN THE CHRIST CHURCH BOG!

Anyway, the statue probably isn't Strongbow's son – it's more likely to be the Earl of Drogheda.

Did you know...?
The first Church of England service was held in the 1540s in Christ Church Cathedral, opposite the Castle. The Irish Catholics came up with a brilliant plot to wreck the service.

There was a marble statue of Jesus in the church with a crown of thorns on his head. They set up some hidden tubes. When the Protestant bishop began to preach, the tubes had blood pumped into them and the marble crown seemed to pour blood down the statue's face.

The people were amazed.

IT'S A SIGN FROM GOD! HE DOESN'T WANT HENRY VIII'S PRIESTS IN HERE!

Dublin quick quiz

Are you a city superbrain or a Dublin dipstick? Try this quiz and find out...

1 The word 'quiz' was invented by a Dublin theatre owner. How did it happen?

a) He wanted to have a 'Question competition' at his theatre. But he was drunk and told everyone it was a 'Quiz-tune competition'!

b) He invented it for a bet.

c) He was playing Scrabble and the letters in the word 'quiz' give a very high score – so he put it on the board and said there really was such a word.

2 Saint Brigid was a famous Irish Saint. A 'relic' she left behind is in Dublin Museum. But what is it?

a) a brass and silver shoe

b) her big toe

c) a handkerchief with her holy snot

3 In 1171 the Normans were in control of Dublin but were attacked by a Viking force of King Hasculf. The Viking warrior was the mighty what?

a) John the Bad

b) John the Sad

c) John the Mad

4 In 1349 a lot of Dublin people were killed by what?

a) trees

b) fleas

c) bees

5 In Elizabeth I's times Shane O'Neill was a wanted man. There was a reward for his head and in 1567 it ended up on Dublin Castle walls. How?
a) Somebody found his corpse in a grave and lopped off the dead head.
b) He lost his head in a vicious game of Gaelic football.
c) He was beheaded in Dublin Castle.

6 Dubliner Kit Welsh served for 20 years in the British army from 1692, was badly wounded four times and was given four medals for bravery by Queen Anne. Why was that unusual?
a) In his first day in the army he blew off his right hand when his gun exploded.
b) He was a woman who went into battle in trousers – well he would have looked silly in a pink flowery frock.
c) He was scared of loud bangs and ran away every time he fired his own gun.

7 In 1787 the police were called to a riotous party in Merrion Square in Dublin. The police didn't do a very good job. Why not?

a) They had locked their truncheons in the police station and they lost the key.

b) Their helmets had all been sent away to be cleaned.

c) Many of them were drunk as kippers.

8 In 1734 the students of Trinity College in Dublin hated their head, Dean Edward Forde. What did they do to show their hatred?

a) They threw him in the river Liffey.

b) They shot him because he asked for it.

c) They put nails through the seat of his chair so when he sat down he got a real pain in the bum.

9 In the 1798 rebellion the rebels hoped to attack Dublin in the dark. But Dublin was lit by gas lamps. How did they plan to put them all out?

a) blow up the gas works

b) get the lamp-lighting men to go on strike

c) get the Dublin kids to smash the gas lamps with stones

10 In 1922 James Joyce wrote Dublin's most famous book. Clever man. But he was not so nice to his poor old dad. What did he call him? (And do NOT copy him even if you do want to become a famous writer.)

a) the silliest man I ever knew

b) the ugliest man I ever knew

c) the smelliest man I ever knew

Answers:

1b) Richard Daly, a theatre owner in Dublin, made a bet that in just two days he could bring a new word into the English language. After the evening show, Mr Daly gave cards to all his staff with the word written on it, and told them to write it on walls all over the city. So 'quiz' came into the language.

2a) Brigid was a cowherd until she met St Patrick and went on to be a top nun in Kildare. She had some clever tricks.

She could turn water into beer which is a BAD thing, of course. If she did it today she would put the Guinness factory in Dublin out of work.

Why would she leave behind a single brass and silver shoe? Where's the other one? On her foot? Does she have to hop in Heaven?

The Dublin museum also has St Kieran's walking staff. It was probably stolen from him by a schoolteacher …

3c) John the Mad was so powerful he would attack Norman knights in their armour. His battle-axe could slice through the Norman rider's leg so the leg fell off one side of the horse and the dead man fell off the other side. He chopped twenty Norman legs that way. Twenty Normans would never play football again.

But another group of Normans sneaked up behind John the Mad and killed him. Viking King Hasculf was captured. Did he say, 'Sorry, lads! You beat me fair and square. I'll get back to my home in the Hebrides'?

No, he didn't. He said...

We only came with a small army this time. Next time I'll be back with a force that will destroy you.

The Normans executed him.

WHY CAN'T I KEEP MY BIG MOUTH SHUT?

4b) Fleas, because fleas spread the plague – 'The Black Death'. It killed almost half of the people of Dublin.

You don't want to know this if you're eating your tea, but here's how the plague spread...

- A flea carries plague germs in its stomach.
- The flea bites a human but it doesn't just suck the blood.
- It vomits some of its germy stomach juices into the wound.
- The germs get into the human's blood and kill him or her.
- The flea hops off to find another victim because fleas don't like dead bodies.

I'M OUT'A HERE!

5a) Shane was murdered and buried at Cushendun, on the Antrim coast and the reward of 1,000 marks was forgotten.

But no sooner was he in the ground than an English soldier, Captain Piers, remembered the reward. He had Shane's corpse dug up and the head cut off. It was put in a pot and pickled and sent to Dublin.

Piers claimed the reward and was given it! The head was stuck on a pike over Dublin Castle walls.

6b) Kit Welsh was a Dublin woman. Her secret wasn't discovered till she retired.

7c) Councillor Exshaw of Dublin Council was walking in Merrion Square on a Sunday when he saw a shocking sight: 'A great number of people, leaping, wrestling and shouting.' Really they were just having a good time! But pompous Exshaw was furious…

The police were called from their Sunday day off and many of them were as drunk as the mob. They had rifles with bayonets on the end. The Dublin Member of Parliament Richard Griffith arrived and told Exshaw:

So what had been a party turned into a riot. The mob threw stones at the police who staggered away…

Who got the blame? Not Exshaw or his drunken police. It was MP Richard Griffith! Some people said he should have been hanged for starting the riot.

He wasn't.

8b) The students stoned Dean Forde's windows so he fired a gun at them. The students ran off – to get their guns! When they returned they fired back and shot him dead.

9b) They told the lamp-lighters to go on strike. Not a bright idea – not as bright as a gas lamp anyway. The lamp-lighters SAID they were on strike but soldiers with bayonets on the end of their guns forced the men to light the gas.

The attackers arrived anyway. There were just 80 of them … and they only brought one ladder to climb the walls of Dublin Castle.

The rebellion failed … but you probably guessed that. Just five years later the rebels were back. There is a story that in 1803 a United Irishmen rebel group went to their boss and asked…

CAN WE HAVE TIME OFF WORK, SIR, TO ATTACK DUBLIN CASTLE?

The boss reported them to the British Army, who arrested them.

That rebellion failed too … and I'll bet you guessed that as well!

10a) Joyce's book is called *Ulysses* and rambles on for hundreds of pages about one day in the life of Dublin.

It is hard to read. Try it some time if you are on a desert island for five years with nothing else to do. Here are a couple of lines…

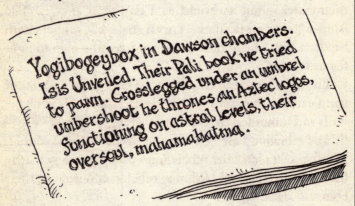

Yogibogeybox in Dawson chambers. Isis Unveiled. Their Pali book we tried to pawn. Crosslegged under an umbrel umbershoot he thrones an Aztec logos, functioning on astral levels, their oversoul, mahamahatma.

Understand that? Clever you.

Joyce's Dublin day was 16 June. Every year, on that day, the fans of Joyce follow his ramble round the streets and bars of Dublin. They dress as the characters in the book – characters like Leopold Bloom, the hero.

It's called 'Bloomsday'.

I MAY BE FINISHED BY DOOMSDAY!

TUDOR AND STUART DUBLIN

The terrible Tudors didn't bother to visit Ireland during their reign but that didn't stop them spilling Irish blood and wrecking Irish futures.

1487 Ireland invades England and their new Tudor King Henry VII. A fake prince (real name Lambert Simnel) says he's really King of England. He's crowned in Christ Church Cathedral and his supporters set sail for England. They are smashed at the battle of Stoke by Henry VII.

1534 The 'Geraldine' Rebellion is led by Lord Thomas Offaly against Henry VIII. 'Silken' Thomas is ruling Ireland for the English King but decides to rebel. Tom rampages through Dublin and tries to take the Castle. But the people of Dublin rise against him and he is defeated. He goes to England for the chop.

1558–1603 Reign of Elizabeth I. Elizabethan 'Plantation' begins: the English give land in Catholic Northern Ireland to Protestants. This will lead to hundreds more years of trouble. Elizabeth has Catholic priests tortured and executed. Dublin becomes the site of many of these executions.

1590 Owen Roe O'Neill, an Irish chieftain's son, is captured and locked in Dublin Castle. But with the help of a long rope he climbs out of the window and escapes. When he is betrayed and caught he is brought back. This time he's kept in chains, but he escapes again the next year and becomes a leading rebel.

1607 Flight of the 'Wild Geese' – the top Irish rulers give up the fight against the English and go to Europe.

1649 Oliver Cromwell, governor of England, lands in Dublin then goes on to invade Ireland. His cruelty will be remembered for a l-o-n-g time. Dublin does not suffer as much as other towns though.

1661 Charles II is welcomed back to the English throne with parties, fireworks and parades in Dublin. No more Cromwell cruelty.

1688 James II is thrown off the English and Scottish thrones for being a Catholic. He decides to run to Dublin and fight for Ireland. The English follow him and attack. He runs off to France. Ireland defeated again.

1704 More new laws mean Catholics can't vote or join the army. They are the under-class, the peasants.

Hanging Henry

In 1538 King Henry VIII told the Irish to stop following the Pope and his Catholic religion and start believing in Henry's new Church of England and the Protestant religion.

The Pope urged the Irish to rebel. He gave a letter to a monk, Thady O'Brian, to take to the Irish. O'Brian was locked in Dublin Castle while Henry decided what to do with him.

Henry ordered that O'Brian should be hanged. O'Brian cheated Henry of his hanging – the monk hanged himself in his castle cell.

The corpse of O'Brian was taken to Gallows Green and hanged there anyway. It was left to rot for a few days. Henry's message was…

Sick Sir Henry's war

Queen Elizabeth I sent Sir Henry Sidney to rule Ireland for her from Dublin.

He wasn't happy just ruling – he had to bring terror to the Irish. Sir Humphrey Gilbert described Henry's horrible habit…

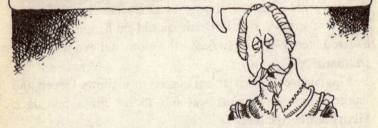

> *His order was that the heads of all those which were killed in the day should be cut off. The heads were to be brought to the place where he camped at night and should there be laid on the ground by each side of the path leading into his tent. So that no one could come into his tent without passing through the lane of heads. This brought great terror to the people when they saw the heads of their dead fathers, brothers, children, relatives and friends lying on the ground before their faces.*

Of course the English soldiers played follow-my-leader and copied his cruelty. A report from Ireland said…

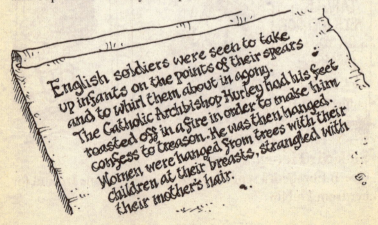

English soldiers were seen to take up infants on the points of their spears and to whirl them about in agony. The Catholic Archbishop Hurley had his feet roasted off in a fire in order to make him confess to treason. He was then hanged. Women were hanged from trees with their children at their breasts, strangled with their mother's hair.

During a rebellion, Irish troops were led into battle by a harp player. So the orders went out from England…

Other English, like Sidney, were also pretty good at cheating. They would:
• invite their Irish enemies to dinner
• disguise their soldiers as servants
• when the enemies sit down to eat, have them stabbed to death.

Seventeen Irish leaders died that way.

The English Earl of Essex used a different trick on Irish rebel leader Sir Brian O'Neill. He…
• went to dinner with Sir Brian
• took his bodyguard
• enjoyed the dinner and waited till Sir Brian and his guards had gone to bed
• massacred all the servants in the house
• arrested the sleepy Sir Brian.

Sir Brian O'Neill and his wife were sent off to Dublin to be executed.

The massacre of 1641

In 1607 the Irish lords just packed up and left Ireland – no one is really sure why! It is known as 'The Flight of the Earls'.

From 1609 the earls' lands were taken over by the English and Scottish farmers.

The poor Irish didn't have a chance to get some land of their own.

Trouble was slow in coming. Thirty years in fact.

There were bad harvests in 1640. And that led to bad tempers. So some of the peasants put together a plot. On 23 October 1641 they planned to kill the Protestants in Ireland. Not just the priests or the ones who went to church. Not just the English and Scottish landowners who made them work. ALL of the Protestants.

Dublin escaped the worst – they had a warning that the rebels were about to strike and the Protestants shut themselves in Dublin Castle. Outside thirty years of hatred was boiling over.

The Protestants later told the most horrific tales. One writer said…

> *No age, man, woman or child, was spared. The wife was killed as she wept for her butchered husband. As she held her helpless children she was pierced with them, and died by the same stroke.*

The writer claimed that Catholic children attacked the dead bodies of their little Protestant playmates. He said the women were as ruthless as the men.

Dire Dubliners 4:
Silken Thomas (1513–1537)
Fact you need to know

His real name was Lord Offaly. His horses wore silk fringes to show they were part of his army. That's how he got the name 'Silken' Thomas.

Terrible Tom was a rebel against Henry VIII. Horrible Henry arrested his dad and Silken Thomas heard Henry had executed him. (He hadn't.)

Tom rode into Dublin at the head of his army and threw down Henry's sword in St Mary's Abbey. The sword was the sign that Tom ruled Ireland for Henry. The message was clear…

The Archbishop of Dublin was an enemy of Tom so he decided it would be a good idea to scoot off to safety in England. He jumped on a boat in the river Liffey and sailed out of Dublin.

Yes, the ship ran aground and the Archbishop had to go ashore and hide in a friend's house. Tom's men found him. A bloody report described what happened next.

> # Silken Thomas handed him over to his supporters, who brained him and hacked him in gobbets

Horrible Histories odd facts: Some English were forced to fight for Thomas. They fired arrows into Dublin Castle … but made sure there were no heads on the arrows so no one was hurt!

They also wrapped messages round the arrows telling the defenders of Thomas's plans.

Henry VIII sent Lord Leonard Grey to Ireland with an army. Tom offered to surrender if Grey would spare his life. Grey said, 'Yes.'

Tom surrendered.

Henry VIII said, 'No. Execute him!'

Silken Thomas was hanged then beheaded and cut into quarters, and the bits were stuck on poles to teach other rebels a lesson.

Did you know…?

Thomas's family name was Thomas Fitzgerald. He started carving his name on the wall of his cell at the Tower of London. He got as far as 'Thomas Fitzgera…' then stopped. It's hard to finish carving your name when you've been cut into quarters!

CRIME AND PUNISHMENT

All big cities like Dublin have creepy criminals, mad murderers and cruel crooks in their history. And most of them, like Dublin, have had some really rotten ways of punishing the villains…

Terrible torture

In 1581 Dermot Hurley, Archbishop of Cashel, had a really nasty time.

He was accused of being a traitor and taken to Dublin Castle. The judges wrote to Queen Elizabeth's ministers to ask:

Dear Your Majesty

Please can we send Dermot Hurley to the Tower of London. He refuses to talk and betray his friends. We think he needs to be tortured and we don't have one of your clever rack thingies to stretch him.

I look forward to hearing from you by return galleon.

Lord Deputy Perrot

The Castle got an answer they didn't expect...

> **My Lord**
>   Our experts suggest you place
> the Archbishop's feet in metal boots
>   and roast them over a fire.
>   Sir Francis Walsingham
>   Secretary of State

The Dublin torturers took the idea and went one better.

FIRST MAKE A METAL BOOT TO FIT THE PRISONER'S LEG

PLACE THE LEG IN THE BOOT AND FILL IT WITH OIL AND SALT

NOW HEAT THE METAL BOOT OVER A FIRE UNTIL THE PRISONER TALKS

REMOVE THE LEG (THE BOOT AND OIL IS A SUPER WAY TO COOK CHIPS TOO!)

Dermot cried out in pain, 'Jesus, son of David, have mercy on me.' But he DIDN'T betray his friends.

He fainted and the torturers were worried he might die.

They took off the boots. As they came off they peeled away the flesh from his legs as well.

He was put back in his filthy cell and the Castle again wrote to the Queen to ask what they could do next.

The Queen wrote back to say she was pleased with the torture but now they should just hang him.

Dermot was secretly taken out at dawn, and hanged with a band of twisted twigs on the gibbet near St Stephen's Green.

His body was buried by some friends in St Kevin's churchyard.

Did you know…?

Prisoners had to PAY to be held in Dublin Castle prison. If they had no money then they were given the poorest food.

One of the prisoners who was in Dublin Castle at the same time as Dermot was widow Eleanor Ball. The Mayor of Dublin had the 77-year-old woman arrested for having a Catholic service in her own home.

She suffered for three years before she died.

Was the Mayor sorry? He should have been.

Eleanor Ball was his mother!

Flattened friar

Father James O'Hea was a Catholic Friar, captured by Queen Elizabeth's Protestant soldiers in the 1590s.

He was thrown into a damp cellar in Dublin Castle and weighed down with chains. There were so many chains he couldn't lift a hand to feed himself. Just to tease him the soldiers placed a bowl of food in front of him.

HMMM... STRAWBERRY TRIFLE!

And to make it extra nasty his wounds weren't treated for a month.

He was to spend more than two years in prison before he was released … alive!

And Father O'Hea was lucky!

Did you know…?
Conor O'Devany was a Franciscan friar and bishop.

In 1612, aged nearly 80, he was accused of treason.

His punishment was to be publicly hung in Dublin, have his guts pulled out before he was dead and then be cut into quarters.

The large Catholic crowd felt sorry for him, of course, but they pushed and jostled each other to get scraps of his clothing or dip cloths in his blood.

They didn't just do this after he was dead – they did it while he was being executed.

Foul fire

There was a trial in the King's Court in Dublin in the early 1700s. A chimney caught fire in a house near the court. Smoke began to drift into the court – disaster followed...

Only Justice Whitshed stayed in his seat and refused to join the panic.

Dire Dubliners 5:
Grace O'Malley (1530–1597)

Facts you need to know

• Grace was born into a family of Irish sailors and pirates.

• She married the vicious Donal O'Flaherty – it was said he murdered his sister's stepson when he thought the boy was getting too much power.

Facts you don't want to know

• Grace wanted to be a pirate like the rest of her family. Her father told the young girl…

Grace was furious. She dressed like a boy and hacked her hair till it was short as a sailor's. She told her father she was ready to sail with him. Her family laughed and gave her a new nickname: Grainne Mhaol (Grace the Bald).

Her father gave in and they set sail for Spain.

On the way they were attacked by an English ship. Her father told her to get safely below the decks. Instead, she climbed up a mast. From her perch she spotted an enemy creeping up behind her father with a knife raised.

Grace dropped on to the man's back, kicking, biting and screaming. The terrified man fled and so did the rest of the English.

She had saved her father's life.

• In 1566 she went to sea when she was expecting a baby. Just as the baby was born, her ship was attacked by Turkish pirates.

The crew didn't know what to do and they ran to her asking for help. She screamed at them…

So Grace put the baby down, grabbed a 'blunderbuss' pistol and went on deck.

They didn't just escape from the Turkish pirates ... they climbed on board the Turkish ship, murdered the crew and took the ship for themselves.

Horrible Histories odd fact: In 1577 Grace was captured by the English and taken to Dublin for trial. The judge said...

> *You are a woman who has spent the best part of her wicked life leading a band of thieves and murderers at sea.*

She was sent to the dungeon of Dublin Castle. Not many people came out of there alive. Yet after a year Grace was set free! She returned to pirate life and died in 1603, a pirate to the end.

Dublin Castle

Most castles are creepsome and Dublin Castle is no different. In its time it's had blood, fire and even Blood!

Pesky Prince
In 1185 Prince John arrived in Dublin and he was Trouble. His lords made fun of the Irish chiefs by pulling their beards. The fashion in England was to shave your face – especially if you were a  man. (The women didn't bother so much.) The Irish chiefs wore beards. John's knights teased them by tugging their beards.

The Irish chiefs were furious and became rebels. The English had to build Dublin Castle to protect their people.

Painful picnic
On Easter Monday 1209 the people of Dublin went off to Ranelagh for a holiday trip and a bit of a picnic.

The bad O'Byrne tribe and the terrible O'Tooles swooped down on the families and chopped them like cucumbers in a picnic sandwich.

Five hundred died and the English had to bring more soldiers from Bristol to help defend Dublin Castle.

The day became known as 'Black Monday'. Every year on 'Black Monday', the Dublin people would march out of the city to the spot where the massacre had happened. They would raise a black banner to the mountains to challenge...

Even 400 years later the people of Dublin were guarding their city walls against the people they called 'the mountain enemy'.

A castle built, a city wall built and five hundred years of fear … all because of a few pulled beards!

Conor O'Connell's cut throat

In 1583 two Irish chieftains decided to settle a quarrel by a fight to the death – mortal combat.

This was the last such contest in Ireland and it would have made sensational reading if there had been newspapers in 1583! Just imagine it…

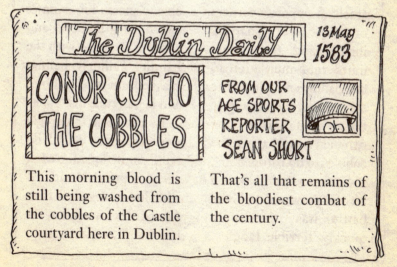

The Dublin Daily 13 May 1583

CONOR CUT TO THE COBBLES

FROM OUR ACE SPORTS REPORTER SEAN SHORT

This morning blood is still being washed from the cobbles of the Castle courtyard here in Dublin.

That's all that remains of the bloodiest combat of the century.

Crowds turned out yesterday to watch two feuding O'Connells settle their differences once and for all. In the red corner was Tadgh and in the blue was Conor. Each man wore just a shirt and a helmet. Each was armed with just a sword and shield.

Before the bitter battle began the furious fighters were searched for hidden weapons – but it's pretty difficult to hide a weapon when you're wearing just a shirt. They sat on small stools in opposite corners of the yard, snarling insults and threatening murderous mutilation to one another. Then the constable of the castle gave the trumpet signal and the two men rushed across the cobbles to do battle.

Some spectators were a bit disappointed that the battle was over quite quickly. Terrible Tadgh chopped Conor's legs and cut him twice. The loss of blood soon weakened the woeful warrior and Tadgh took pity on Conor. He lowered his sword and Conor took the chance to slash Tadgh in the ribs.

THE UPPER CUT

The furious Tadgh was able to snatch his enemy's sword, turn it round and batter at his head with the handle. Conor's helmet crashed on the cobbles and it was curtains.

By this time the crowd were screaming 'Kill! Kill! Kill!' So he killed. Tadgh sliced Conor's head off with his own sword then passed the head to his family.

Today Conor's family were on their knees praying for his soul, while Dublin Castle cleaners were on their knees scrubbing. 'It'll take days to clean this mess up,' Mrs Molly O'Mopp moaned.

The Great Fire

In the Great Fire of 1684 Dublin Castle was ruined.

It started around one o'clock in the morning.

The Duke of Ormond's son, James Butler, heard crackling flames as the floorboards of his room caught alight.

He ran for his life. The soldiers blew up part of the Castle to stop the flames spreading but it didn't work.

Stories went around Dublin at the time and they said the fire was NOT an accident. They said it was started by James Butler on purpose!

King James (in England) said...

THE FIRE AT DUBLIN CASTLE WAS AN ACCIDENT!

He probably said this to protect Butler, but did the Butler do it? We'll never know...

Dire Dubliners 6:
Thomas Blood (1617–1680)

Fact you need to know

Blood was a violent and greedy criminal who almost got away with the craziest plots in Britain.

Blood was born in Ireland but in 1660 lost some of his lands when Charles II became king. He decided he wanted:

The plot was to grab Dublin Castle and kidnap the governor, Lord Ormond. It would work like this...

Sounds like a good plan to take over your school, kidnap the head and get off that 10-hour detention! But what went wrong?

One of Blood's friends was really a Castle spy. Many of the gang were arrested and hanged. Blood failed to save them from the gallows and ran off to England where he had an even crazier plot. So crazy it almost worked!

In 1671 Thomas Blood plotted to steal the Crown Jewels from the Tower of London.

Blood…

• made friends with the keeper of the Crown Jewels, Talbot Edwards
• arranged for Talbot's daughter to marry his nephew, then…
• …on the day of the wedding his wedding guests asked to see the jewels.

Talbot led them down to the jewel room where they jumped on him and…

• …kept him quiet with a lump of wood stuffed in his mouth
• stole the jewels and rode off on a waiting horse but…

• …crashed his getaway horse into a cart and was caught.

CURSES… CART IN THE ACT!

Everyone expected Thomas Blood to hang. Instead he was set free AND given his lands in Ireland!

It seems he may have betrayed his old rebel friends and done a deal with King Charles.

Horrible Histories odd fact: Blood died of a fever in 1680. A story went around that he had faked his death. His body had to be dug up to PROVE he really WAS dead.

GEORGIAN TO TWENTIETH CENTURY TIMELINE

1798 The United Irishmen plan a rising against the English, led by Wolfe Tone. Thirty thousand people die in the rebellion. Tone is captured and sent to be executed but cuts his throat just before they can hang him in Dublin.

1801 Ireland loses its Parliament and is ruled by the British Parliament in Westminster. The Union Jack was first flown not in England but over Dublin, on 1 January 1801, to celebrate the Act of Union which said Ireland would be ruled by the Parliament in London. Ireland could have 100 Members of Parliament … so long as none was a Catholic. Could be trouble!

1803 United Irishmen rise again, this time led by 24-year-old Robert Emmet. Only about 80 join in. Emmet is tried and executed.

1845–49 The Great Famine occurs when the potato crops fail four years in a row. Millions starve or are forced to leave Ireland. Queen Victoria visits Dublin and claims…

THIS WOLFE IS NOT GOING TO THE DOGS!

IS THAT A UNION JACK?

I DON'T KNOW AND MY NAME'S NOT JACK!

IRELAND AND ITS PEOPLE ARE DELIGHTFUL

THAT'S ALL RIGHT THEN, FAT VIC LIKES US. WE CAN FORGET ABOUT THE FAMINE!

1866 The 'Fenians' start to make trouble now. They want Ireland to be free from British rule.

1882 The English Lord Cavendish is murdered in Phoenix Park and Dublin troubling is a worry for the Brits.

1916 The Easter Rising. The Irish Republican Brotherhood join the Irish Citizen Army to throw out the British. Dublin sees most of the blood-soaked trouble. They fail. The leaders are executed in May and now most Irish want to be free of English rule.

1922 The Irish Free State is formed with Dublin as the capital. Six northern Irish states don't want to join so they stay as part of Britain.

Rotten rebels

In 1803 Robert Emmet led a rebellion. But he was shocked as he watched his followers catch the kindly Lord Kilwarden and slash him to death with a pike in Patrick Street.

Emmet fired a signal rocket to tell his rebels to stop the killing. Then he ran off to the Wicklow mountains to hide.

He could have got away with it but he was desperate to see his girlfriend, Sarah Curran. He came out of hiding and was arrested. Emmet was taken to be executed outside St Catherine's Church in Thomas Street.

A song, written after his death, says…

BOLD ROBERT EMMET,
THE DARLING OF IRELAND.
BOLD ROBERT EMMET,
WILL DIE WITH A SMILE.

In fact, he did not die quite like a true Irish hero. Emmet told the hangman …

DO NOT TAKE THE LADDERS AWAY UNTIL I DROP THIS HANDKERCHIEF

…but he wouldn't drop it! In the end the hangman grew fed up with Emmet saying, 'Not yet!' and he pushed him off…

I HAVEN'T DROPPED MY HANDKER… CHOKE!

SHOVE!

ABOUT TIME!

Did you know…?

A song was written about Emmet, but in the song he became a drake – a fine male duck – that was stolen from an Irish girl, Nell Flaherty.

In the song she curses the people that stole her lovely friend.

You may like to use this curse against the school bully and see if it works!

May his pig never grunt, may his cat never hunt,
May a ghost always haunt him in the dead of the night,
May his hen never lay, may his ass never bray,
May his coat fly away like an old paper kite;

May the lice and the fleas the wretch ever tease,
May the pinching north breeze make him tremble and shake,
May a four-year-old bug build a nest in the lug,
Of the monster that murdered Nell Flaherty's drake.

May his pipe never smoke, may his teapot be broke,
And to add to the joke may his kettle not boil,
May he lay in the bed 'til the moment he's dead
May he always be fed on lob-scouse and fish oil,

May he swell with the gout, may his back teeth fall out,
May he roar, bawl and shout, with the horrid toothache.
May his duck never quack, and his goose turn quite black
The monster that murdered Nell Flaherty's drake.

May his spade never dig, may his sow never pig,
Every nit on his head be as large as a snail,
May his house have no thatch and his door have no latch,
May his turkey not hatch, may the rats eat his meal,

May his dog yelp and growl with hunger and cold,
And everyone curse him asleep or awake,
May weasels still gnaw him, and jackdaws still claw him,
So this ends the song of Nell Flaherty's drake.

Dire Dubliners 7:
Sarah Malcolm (1711–1733)

Fact you need to know

Savage Sarah was a throat-slitting, blood-splashing servant who wanted money from her neighbour, Widow Duncomb.

Facts you don't want to know

The old widow shared a house with two maids, old Betty and young Anne.

One February morning in 1733 Anne was found with her throat cut from ear to ear. Betty and Widow Duncomb had been strangled.

Sarah was blamed.

Her apron was found under her bed and was covered with blood, while her bloody dress was found stuffed down the toilet.

Then 45 gold coins were found and they proved she was a thief. Where were the coins found?

a) in her mouth

b) in her hair

c) in her knickers

Answer: b) Sarah's hair would have been thick and greasy and tied up on her head. She would be able to hide the coins along with the head lice.

Horrible Histories odd facts:

• Sarah was sent to be hanged and looked very smart in a black dress and black gloves. Hundreds of people turned out to see her so platforms were built to give the crowds a really good view.

• The rickety platforms collapsed and dozens of people were hurt. But not as hurt as Sarah when they hanged her, of course. She was standing on a cart and a rope was put round her neck. The cart was then driven away.

• Sarah was UNLUCKY! She said that she planned to rob the house but Anne woke up and struggled so she killed her. The struggle woke the other two and she had to kill them as well.

• Sarah was LUCKY! If she had been Widow Duncomb's servant she would NOT have been hanged – the punishment for a servant killing her mistress was to be burned alive at the stake.

A FEW FOUL PLACES TO VISIT

There are lots of interesting places to visit in Dublin but do you want to know their HORRIBLE stories?

St Stephen's Green Square
This pretty park is a pleasant place for a picnic, but it used to be a place of pain. On 30 November 1765 a rich merchant, Captain Glas, sailed to Ireland. Four local pirates heard about the treasure onboard so that night they rowed out to the ship.

They murdered Captain Glas with his own sword and threw his body overboard. Then they killed the crew. Captain Glas's wife and 11-year-old daughter followed.

The murderers went to Dublin and spent their fortune, which was a stupid thing to do. They were arrested and taken to St Stephen's Green where they were hanged in public.

The bodies were put on show, hanging by the edge of the river Liffey. But, when they started to rot, people complained and they were moved to Dalkey Island so people sailing into Dublin could see them and be warned: this is what Dublin does to pirates.

75

St Stephen's Green was also a nice place to go to watch whippings and people being burned. Just don't go there and expect it to be so exciting today.

Did you know…?
St Stephen's Green isn't square. It's an oblong. Of all the Dublin 'squares' only Mountjoy Square is square.

Did you also know…?
The world's most famous park is probably New York's Central Park. But its layout was copied from St Stephen's Green.

Kilmainham Jail
This jail has been the 'home' of rebels from 1798 to 1924.

It was the last home for many rebels who were executed inside the grim and grimy walls.

It's a museum now and you can see the hanging room and also the exercise yard. That's the spot where the leaders of the 1916 Easter Rising were executed by a British firing squad.

The only 'exercise' they got was walking to the wall … they didn't have to walk back.

Rebel leader James Connolly didn't even get to walk to the wall. He was shot sitting in a chair as he was too weak from a gunshot injury.

Donnybrook

This used to be a village on the road out of Dublin but now it's part of Dublin.

In 1204 King John gave Donnybrook the right to have a fair. (Buying and selling things, not a swings and roundabouts sort of fair.)

Each year it started on 26 August and went on for 15 days. It was a meeting-place for horse dealers, fortune-tellers, beggars, wrestlers, dancers, fiddlers and the sellers of every kind of food and drink.

But it soon became famous for a place where the folk of Dublin went to eat, drink, drink a lot more … then fight.

They used heavy wooden clubs they called 'shillelaghs' (say 'shillay-laz'). A Victorian Englishman wrote…

There is only one rule in Donnybrook fights: if you see a head then hit it!

The Irish treated it as more of a joke. An Irish poet imagined Brian Boru went to Donnybrook for a bit of a break:[8]

---

8 Of course King Brian couldn't go to Donnybrook Fair because it hadn't been invented when he was a lad. The boring history books will tell you this. But as this is a *Horrible Histories* book I won't tell you that and spoil the joke.

KING BRIAN BORU WAS A MONARCH SO BOLD,
HE DRESSED COOL IN THE HEAT
AND DRESSED WARM IN THE COLD!
WHEN TIRED OF THE STATE AND ITS TERRIBLE CARE,
OH, HE'D TAKE HIS SHILLELAGH TO DONNYBROOK FAIR!

LIKE ONE OF HIS PEASANTS HE'D JOIN IN THE FUN,
BREAK THE HEADS OF HIS PEOPLE AS IF HE WAS ONE,
AND LOOK SUCH A DARLING THAT NOBODY KNEW
WHETHER HE WAS ST PATRICK OR BRIAN BORU!

The boring old Dublin Council closed the fair in 1855.

Glasnevin Cemetery

A cemetery is one of the top places you may want to visit –
if you are a horrible historian.

Look for the grave of Captain John Boyd[9].

In February 1861 he was a captain of the steam ship
HMS *Ajax*. When three ships were wrecked in a storm off
the coast of Dublin he took his ship out to help them along
with his faithful hound. This dog was a black Newfoundland.

9 You can find his statue in St Patrick's Cathedral, but his grave is a more
interesting sight, as you'll see…

The captain left his ship and climbed onto the pier to help some sailors to safety. A massive wave swept them all to their deaths.

But the black dog was found, drifting, still onboard HMS *Ajax*.

The dog stayed beside his master's coffin during the funeral in St Patrick's Cathedral and all the way to the cemetery at Glasnevin.

He refused any food or water and died on top of the grave.

The haunting hound's ghost can still be seen lying on the grave. (Why can't the ghost of Captain Boyd collect him?)

OH, MY! WAIT TILL I TELL THE FOLKS BACK HOME I TROD IN SOME GHOSTLY DOGGY-DOO!

The General Post Office, O'Connell Street

Post Offices are not usually very exciting places. Maybe the odd pensioner punch-up when a wrinklie gets a foot stamped on? (Post Office – stamp? Oh, never mind.)

But Dublin's Post Office was the place where Irish rebels cried out they were free of British rule – then locked the doors and wouldn't letter anyone in.

The Brit troops of the King set fire to it to get them out. It was royal male against royal mail.

You can still see the bullet scars where the fighting took place.

Dire Dubliners 8:
Billy the Bowl (died 1786)

Facts you need to know

• Billy the Bowl was a beggar. He was born without legs and got around in a metal bowl on wheels. His arms became very powerful.

• Billy was very handsome and made a good living by begging on Dublin streets. But then he became greedy. He spent a lot on drink and gambling and begging didn't pay enough.

Facts you don't want to know

Billy went in for highway robbery. At night he would lie in the bushes by the lonely lanes of Grangegorman and Stoneybatter. He would wait for a woman to come along the lane then cry out for help.

When the woman stuck her head into the bushes he would use his strong arms to choke her – just enough to make her faint.

Billy would pinch her purse then scoot off into the night.

The new Dublin police force was baffled. No one thought the robber could be the legless beggar.

Then one night he met a strong woman who struggled much harder than the others. To keep her quiet he strangled her to death. The police weren't looking for a highway robber anymore. They were hunting a murderer.

The case was known as the 11 Grangegorman Lane Murder.

People came from miles around to look at the place where the murder took place.

Billy kept out of sight until the fuss had died down.

After a few months Billy went back to his robbing ways. Then one night he made a mistake. He attacked a fat cook and she struggled hard. Billy didn't know she had a friend with her. The friend pulled out a long hat-pin and stabbed the robber in the eye. His screams brought the police running and he was arrested.

Horrible Histories odd fact: Some reports say they could never prove Billy was the 11 Grangegorman Lane murderer and he got away with it.

Other reports say he was hanged for his crimes.

NASTY 1916 REBELLION

During Easter 1916 a group called the Irish Republican Brotherhood (the IRB) wanted freedom from Britain. The revolution was meant to happen all over Ireland but in the end it only happened in Dublin.

The workers of Dublin had also formed themselves into a little army of about 250 men and they called themselves 'The Irish Citizen Army'.

The workers' army and the IRB marched into Dublin on Easter Monday 1916. The rebels were supplied with guns from Germany – which was at war with Britain at that time.

The British Army defeated the Irish rebels but Brit General Maxwell decided to execute the rebel leaders.

The dead leaders became heroes, of course.

> SO WERE THOSE 1916 REBELS REALLY HEROES? OR WERE THEY VILLAINS?

It depends on the stories you listen to.

> They were villains, of course.
>   They stole workmen's carts to build barricades – when a harmless workman tried to take his cart away they shot him in the head.

> Cowards

An unarmed policeman at Dublin Castle asked them politely to leave. They shot him in the head.

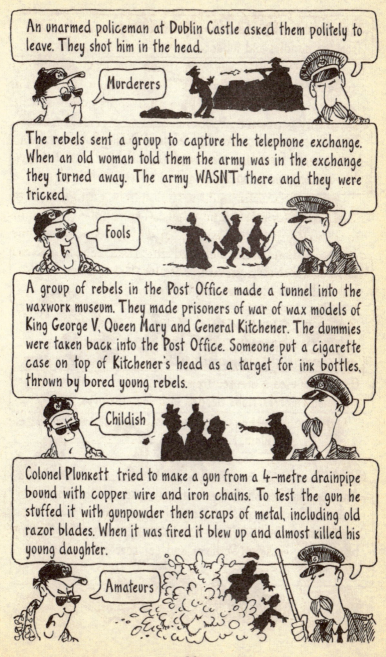

Murderers

The rebels sent a group to capture the telephone exchange. When an old woman told them the army was in the exchange they turned away. The army WASN'T there and they were tricked.

Fools

A group of rebels in the Post Office made a tunnel into the waxwork museum. They made prisoners of war of wax models of King George V, Queen Mary and General Kitchener. The dummies were taken back into the Post Office. Someone put a cigarette case on top of Kitchener's head as a target for ink bottles, thrown by bored young rebels.

Childish

Colonel Plunkett tried to make a gun from a 4-metre drainpipe bound with copper wire and iron chains. To test the gun he stuffed it with gunpowder then scraps of metal, including old razor blades. When it was fired it blew up and almost killed his young daughter.

Amateurs

His men then stuck to making 2 metre-long pikes with heads from tea caddies and tobacco tins.

Daft

The rebels couldn't control the people of Dublin. Mobs went out looting shops. First to go were windows of Noblett's sweet shop. A crowd of women and children fought over sweets in street.

Gluttons

In Saxone shoe shop, drunken women fought over shoes, only to find that boxes contained only left feet.

Idiots

One woman used a wrecked tram car as a changing room to try on looted knickers. Mobs flooded in to loot the pubs.

Villains

Anyway, the British Army wasn't all bad. In the rising at Richmond Barracks, most of the young rebels were set free. They were told by a British officer 'You are thoughtless youths... You've been led by madmen. Go home and get your mothers to wipe your noses.'

Or you could say the rebels were all heroes...

The rebels were heroes, I can tell you.
We were outnumbered. When we started the fighting the British army had three times as many men as the Irish. By the end of a week they had twenty times as many.

Gallant

They did not usually go around murdering their enemies. When they ran into the Post Office, a Brit officer was buying stamps. The first thing he knew was when a rebel poked him in the backside with a pike. He was taken prisoner.

Merciful

The rebels had a sense of humour. Volunteer Joseph Guilfoyle was sent to guard a railway bridge. Rebel leader De Valera told him 'Remember, shoot anything you see in uniform.' Guilfoyle told his friends, 'I just stopped myself from asking if this order included postmen!'.

Funny

The rebels were cruelly killed by better weapons. They dug trenches in St Stephen's Green park. But those trenches were overlooked by the tall Shelbourne Hotel and the rebels were machine-gunned.

Brave

Rebel Private James Fox lost his nerve and ran for the railings at the edge of the park. He was cut down by machine-gun bullets but still crawled on. A second burst killed him. But a British machine-gunner continued to fire at the body. It looked as though Fox was still alive as his body moved under the hammering of bullets.

Victim

Children as young as 8 played at being rebels – with real rifles they picked up – while their mothers sat on a dead horse and watched. They marched to the Post Office, saluted, then fired their guns at the building before running off singing, 'We are the Volunteers, And we'll whack the British Army.'

Popular

After the Easter Holiday the rebels still held the Post Office. Several rebels asked if they could leave. The leader asked, 'Why?' and they told him, 'Because we'll be late for work!'.

Ordinary

And normal life did go on during the rising. The St Stephen's Green park keeper, James Kearney, was allowed into the park twice a day to feed the ducks.

Human

A blind old man appeared on Eden Quay and as he crossed the road a British sniper shot him. The old man fell writhing to the ground. Henry Olds, of the St John's Ambulance Brigade, ran to help him. He bandaged the wound and helped the man back across O'Connell Bridge. The sniper fired twice and both men fell dead.

Courageous

The British didn't know how to fight the Irish women. The women could smuggle weapons inside their clothes or under their skirts. British soldiers were too polite to search them. One officer suggested he could dress up his men as women and they could search suspicious Irish women.

Heroes, every man, woman and child.

VILLAINS?

LOSERS, I GUESS!

HEROES?

The rebels were punished brutally.

They'd seized Dublin Post Office and held it for almost a week before they were captured by the British soldiers.

That's when the Brits made the mistake of the century. They sentenced the surviving rebels to death and had most of them shot in Kilmainham Jail.

The hated Volunteers now became the hero Volunteers! Especially when the people heard horror stories like the execution of their leader, James Connolly, who was dying from his wounds and had to be propped up on a chair so he could be shot. Ordinary people of Dublin shared the suffering of the rebels.

JAMES CONNOLLY

• a nun was killed shutting a convent window;
• a young girl was killed as she stood in her doorway watching the fighting;
• one man raised his hand to wave to a friend and was shot dead by a British soldier who thought he was going to throw a bomb.

All over central Dublin, the dead were buried in back gardens.

The failed 1916 rising turned out to be a curious sort of success. The British were seen as bullies and even peaceful Irish people turned against them. Nobody likes a bully.

After 700 years of trying Ireland would win its freedom in five years.

Dublin would be the capital of the new Irish Free State.

Dead polite people

Even during troubles Dublin people have remained polite. Here are two oddly horrible stories of how pleasant the people can be.

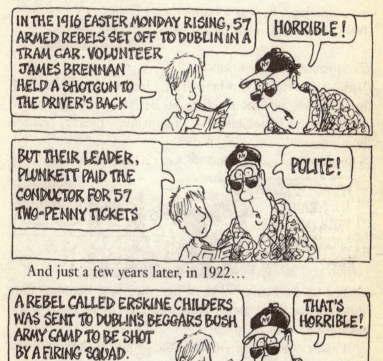

IN THE 1916 EASTER MONDAY RISING, 57 ARMED REBELS SET OFF TO DUBLIN IN A TRAM CAR. VOLUNTEER JAMES BRENNAN HELD A SHOTGUN TO THE DRIVER'S BACK

HORRIBLE!

BUT THEIR LEADER, PLUNKETT PAID THE CONDUCTOR FOR 57 TWO-PENNY TICKETS

POLITE!

And just a few years later, in 1922...

A REBEL CALLED ERSKINE CHILDERS WAS SENT TO DUBLIN'S BEGGARS BUSH ARMY CAMP TO BE SHOT BY A FIRING SQUAD.

THAT'S HORRIBLE!

BUT BEFORE THEY LINED UP CHILDERS WENT TO EACH SOLDIER AND SHOOK HIM BY THE HAND

THAT'S POLITE!

Dire Dubliners 9:
James Carey (1837–1883)

Fact you need to know
When he wasn't setting up assassinations, he was a builder from Denzille Street.

Facts you don't want to know
James was a rich man who believed Ireland should be ruled by the Irish, not the English. So he joined a group called 'The Irish Invincibles' – 'invincible' means 'cannot be beaten'.

The secret Invincibles society went round whispering[10]...

They were being polite. When they said 'remove' they didn't mean send a taxi round to take them away. They meant 'kill'.

The best people to kill were the people at the top of the government.

10 Of course I am only guessing that they whispered. If you were in a secret society you wouldn't go around shouting it, would you?

They then took a pot at the 'Chief Secretary' of the government, W. E. Forster.

James Carey knew where to find Burke. He would be taking a walk in Phoenix Park. On 6 May 1882 Carey showed his assassins who to attack.

As luck would have it Burke was walking with the new Chief Secretary, Lord Cavendish. They attacked both men and stabbed two 'tyrants' to death when they planned to kill one.

The police finally arrested James Carey in January 1883 and was told he'd hang for the murders … unless he told the police who the secret Invincibles were. If James told them then they would hang the Invincibles and set him free.

So what would you do?

So? Which did James Carey do?

He went for B … B for Betrayal. While five of his comrades were hanging in Dublin the cowardly Carey was sailing off to a new life in South Africa.

A lot of Irish Invincibles wanted to see him die, so he travelled with a new name – Power.

Some people would say he got away with murder.

Horrible Histories odd fact: James Carey was the most hated man in Ireland. Mr Power on the South African ship was safe. So it was strange that Mr Power told an Irish shipmate, Patrick O'Donnell:

Not a good idea. Patrick O'Donnell was armed with a gun. He shot Carey dead on 29 July 1883. O'Donnell was taken back to England, tried and executed.

O'Donnell did not get away with murder … and neither did James Carey, of course.

EPILOGUE

If you ever go to Dublin it is useful to have a few facts in your head. Repeat these to Dublin people and they will say…

…or they may say…

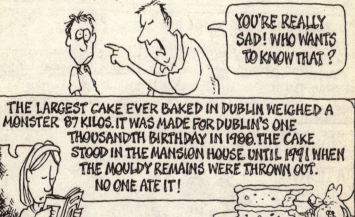

THE CELLARS OF ST MICHAN'S CHURCH IN DUBLIN HAVE THE MOST PERFECTLY PRESERVED CORPSES FROM THE MIDDLE AGES. IT MAY HAVE SOMETHING TO DO WITH THE LIMESTONE WALLS OF THEIR TOMBS.

SWALLOWING A LIVE FROG WAS AN OLD IRISH CURE FOR A STOMACH ACHE. AND IF TEACHER HAS A HANGOVER THEN ONE IRISH CURE IS TO BE BURIED UP TO THE NECK IN DAMP RIVER SAND!

DUBLIN'S O'CONNELL BRIDGE WAS FIRST MADE OF ROPE." IT COULD ONLY CARRY ONE MAN AND A DONKEY AT THAT TIME!

THERE'S A RARE SIGHT - A TIGHTROPE - WALKING DONKEY!

11 It was replaced with a wooden structure in 1801. The modern concrete bridge was built in 1863. O'Connell Bridge is the only traffic bridge in Europe that is wider than it is long.

DUBLIN HAD ITS OWN WEREWOLF LEGENDS. THESE CREATURES WERE THE SOULS OF THE PEOPLE WHO HAD REFUSED TO LISTEN TO THE TEACHINGS OF ST PATRICK!

EVERYONE KNOWS THIS LEGEND, THAT ST PATRICK DROVE ALL THE SNAKES OUT OF IRELAND. BUT NO ONE (EXCEPT HORRIBLE HISTORIES READERS) KNOWS THIS AMAZING FACT...THERE ARE NO MOLES IN IRELAND!

THE FIRST VICTIM OF THE IRISH CIVIL WAR (1922-1923) WAS A FREE STATE GUNMAN WHO WAS SMASHED OVER THE HEAD WITH A TEAPOT BY AN OLD DUBLIN LADY.

CRACK!

NELSON'S PILLAR WAS BLOWN UP IN 1966, THE FIFTIETH BIRTHDAY OF THE 1916 RISING, BECAUSE NELSON WAS AN ENGLISH HERO. IT NOW LIES IN A HEAP IN COUNTY WICKLOW. BUT NELSON'S HEAD IS SAFE IN THE DUBLIN CIVIC MUSEUM.

NELSON

THERE ARE SEVEN AREAS IN DUBLIN WHOSE NAMES END IN THE LETTER 'O'. ONLY ONE DUBLINER IN 20,000 CAN NAME THEM. THEY ARE: MARINO, RIALTO, PORTOBELLO, PHIBSBORO, MONTO, CASINO AND PIMLICO!

Dublin is one of the friendliest cities in the world these days. You can probably visit it without any fear of a Viking chopping you off at the knees.

And old Strongbow is dead so there's less chance of someone chopping you off at the waist!

You probably won't end up locked in chains in Dublin Castle. I doubt if your head will end up on a pole over the castle walls.

But if your head DOES end up there you can be sure of having a lovely view. You can look down on the statue of Molly Malone and the ghosts of Glasnevin Cemetery.

You'll look at such a peaceful scene it will be hard to imagine that thousands of people died dreadfully in Dublin's painful past.

That's Dublin for you. A place with a horrible history, but a history that's a little odd.

I CAN ONLY SAY DUBLIN IS A HORRIBLY ODD PLACE! TIME TO GO HOME!